**Which words or phrases have a similar meaning to the focus word? Write them in the spaces below.**

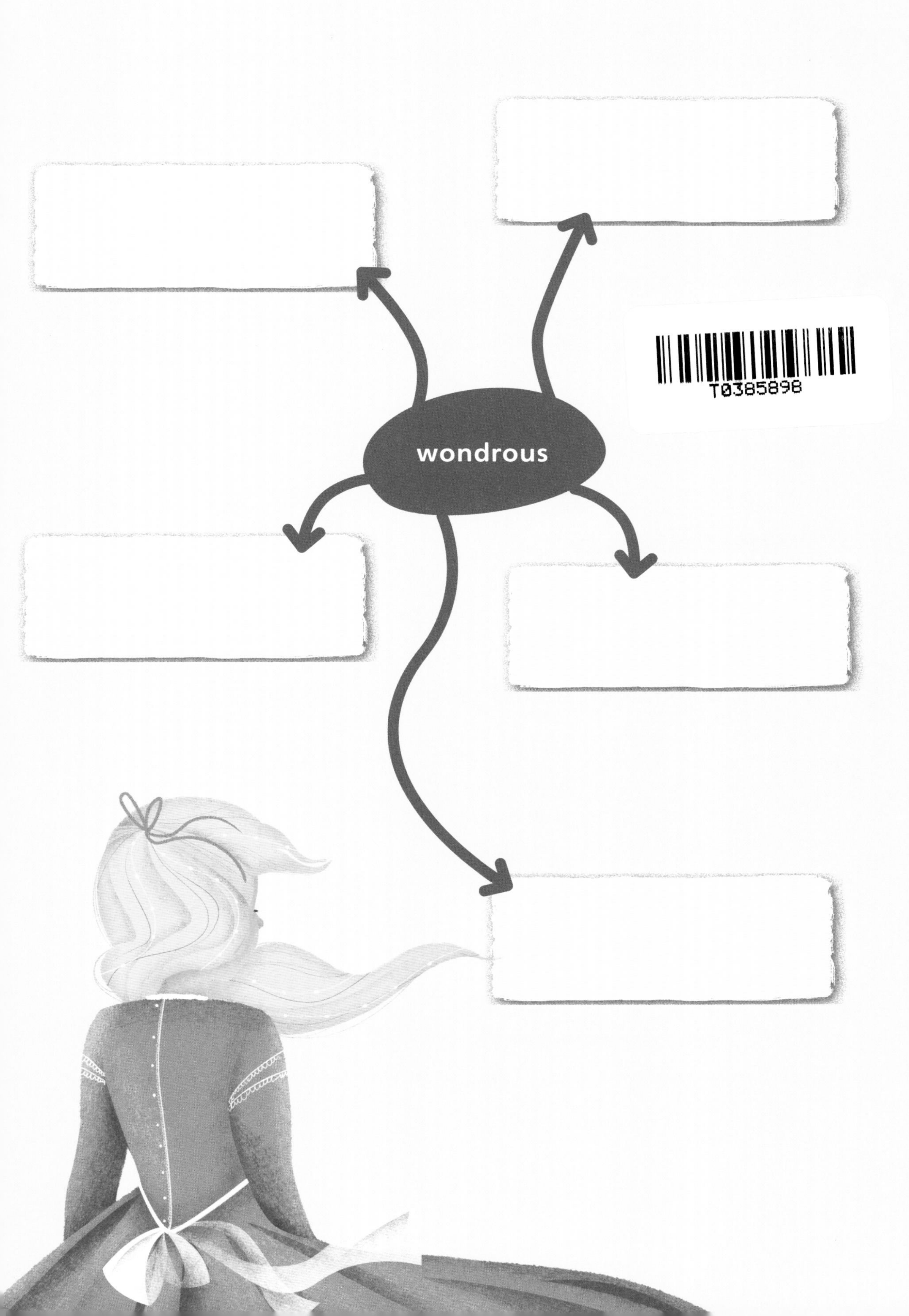

**Read Chapter 1 of *Beyond the Horizon.* Record your thoughts about each of the three questions in the spaces below.**

**The looking question is ...**
Where is Sarah's father going, and how is he getting there?

**The clue question is ...**
Why won't he take Sarah with him?

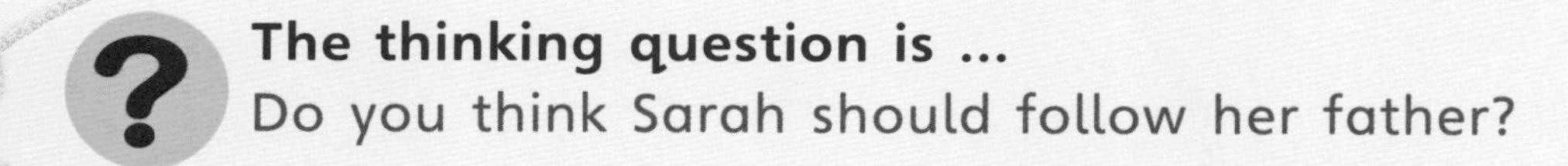

**The thinking question is ...**
Do you think Sarah should follow her father?

**Do you have any questions? Write them here.**

**Think about the conversations you have had about this text. What more have you learned? Complete the activity below.**

Do you think Sarah is foolish to follow her father? Give reasons for your answer.

## Do you think Sarah appeals to the reader?

Write the reasons for your answer below.

**Feedback**

**Use the bold words to write your own sentences in the spaces provided.**

"Very well, then," the cook **relented**.

Her father felt the **burden**.

With **favourable** winds at its back, the *Trades Increase* crossed the Indian Ocean.

Sarah and Cook did what they could to provide good **sustenance** to the men.

## Explore the focus word by completing the activities below.

Look up the focus word in a dictionary and write a definition.

Write an antonym for the focus word.

**proffered**

Write your own sentence using the focus word.

Write a synonym for the focus word.

**Read Chapter 2 of *Beyond the Horizon*. Record your thoughts about each of the three questions in the spaces below.**

**The looking question is …**
How long does the voyage take? Why?

**The clue question is …**
Why does Sarah hide her identity on board the ship?

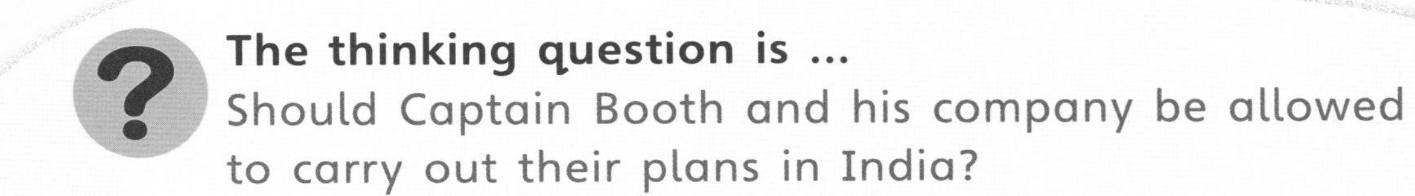

**The thinking question is …**
Should Captain Booth and his company be allowed to carry out their plans in India?

**Do you have any questions? Write them here.**

**Think about the conversations you have had about this text. What more have you learned? Complete the activity below.**

Do you think Sarah's father is right to make the journey to India to set up a trading post, and take what he wants from India?

**Imagine you are Sarah on board the ship. What can you smell, touch, hear, taste and see? Draw or write your answers in the spaces below.**

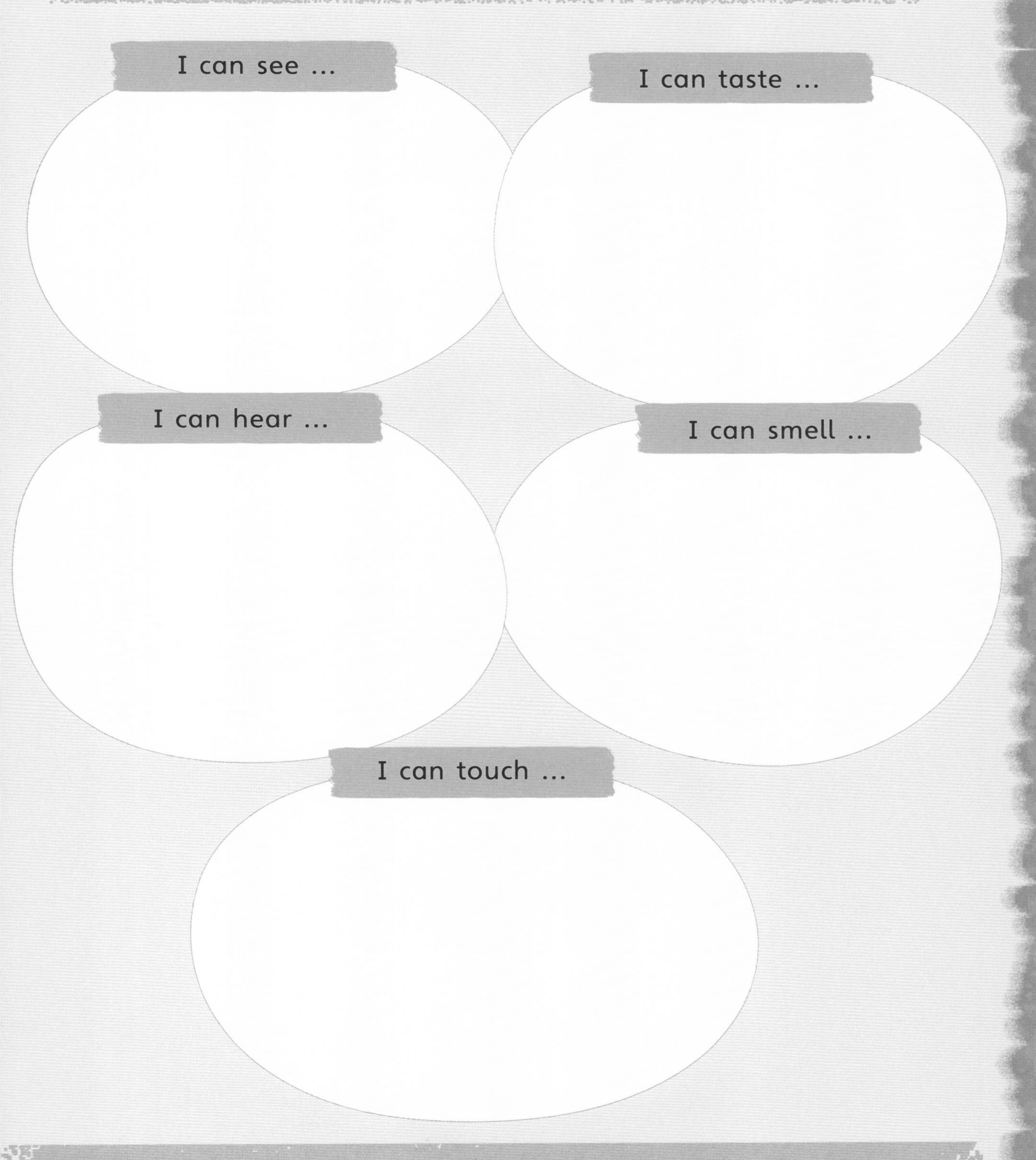


**Feedback**

**Do you know what the words below mean? Record your thoughts about each meaning, then look up the words in a dictionary.**

| Word | I think this word means … | The definition in the dictionary is … |
| --- | --- | --- |
| wharf | | |
| curfew | | |
| reprimanded | | |
| thoroughfare | | |
| haggling | | |

## Put each word into the correct sentence.

**berth fort inlet provisions fare freight**
**pungent merchant turrets**

Mum and Dad packed plenty of ........................ for our camping trip.

"This ........................ is fit for a queen!" she said, sitting down to eat.

High above the castle, soldiers fired arrows from the ........................ .

The children decided to build a ........................ using plastic bricks.

People thought the wealthy ........................ was greedy and selfish.

Grandma's ........................ perfume made me sneeze!

There was only one ........................ left when the boat arrived at the docks.

The two ships could only just pass each other in the narrow ........................ of the river.

The ........................ train slowly made its way up the hill, carrying its heavy load.

**Read Chapter 3 of *Beyond the Horizon*. Record your thoughts about each of the three questions in the spaces below.**

**The looking question is ...**
How does Sarah get lost?

**The clue question is ...**
How do we know that India is a strange place for Sarah?

**The thinking question is ...**
How would you feel if you were Sarah arriving in India?

**Do you have any questions? Write them here.**

**Think about the conversations you have had about this text. What more have you learned? Complete the activity below.**

Imagine you are Sarah. Write a letter to a friend at home, telling them all about the market.

**Summarise what happened in Chapter 3 of *Beyond the Horizon* using the flow chart below.**

What are Sarah and Cook asked to do?

Then where does Cook go?

Who turns up?

How does Sarah get lost?

What happens when she asks for help?

How does the chapter end?

**Feedback**

**Can you remember these words from the previous chapters? Write two sentences using each word in the spaces below.**

**barbarous**

**favourable**

**reprimanded**

**wondrous**

**Draw lines to match the bold word in each sentence to the word or phrase that is closest in meaning. Look up any words you don't know in a dictionary.**

She waited for the test results, full of **anguish**.

He is a troublemaker, but **perchance** he will grow into a fine gentleman.

Dad finally **unravelled** the tangled fairy lights for the party.

The princess worried that the prince had **forsaken** her.

The **lilting** sound of the waves outside sent the boy straight to sleep.

The **silhouette** of the doll looked frightening in the moonlight.

The horse was **tethered** to a gatepost at the edge of the field.

"Rest is the best **remedy** for a bad cold," said Gran.

tied up

pleasant and gentle

dark outline

distress

treatment or cure

abandoned

unwound

perhaps

**Read Chapter 4 of *Beyond the Horizon*. Record your thoughts about each of the three questions in the spaces below.**

**The looking question is ...**
How do Priya and her family show kindness to Sarah?

**The clue question is ...**
How does Sarah's experience differ from her father's view of the people of India?

**The thinking question is ...**
Do you think Sarah would be happy to stay with Priya forever?

**Do you have any questions? Write them here.**

**Think about the conversations you have had about this text. What more have you learned? Complete the activities below.**

If Priya and Sarah spoke the same language, what questions would Priya ask Sarah?

If Priya and Sarah spoke the same language, what questions would Sarah ask Priya?

What do you think Sarah would say to her father about the people of India?

**What do we know about Priya? Write three words to describe Priya and explain why you chose those words in the spaces provided.**

I think Priya is ...

I think this because ...

I think Priya is ...

I think this because ...

I think Priya is ...

I think this because ...

**Feedback**

## Explore the focus word by completing the activities below.

Look up the focus word in a dictionary and write a definition.

Make up a sentence using the focus word.

**revelation**

Write a synonym for the focus word.

Write an antonym for the focus word.

**Put each word into the correct sentence.**

**deserted tarry halt imploring regardless frantically beckoned impatiently**

The heartbroken boy searched .................................... for his favourite toy.

When they arrived, the house was .................................... : everyone had gone!

The car came to a sudden .................................... when a cyclist came out of nowhere.

The strange woman .................................... for us to follow her.

If we .................................... much longer we will be late for the party.

No one noticed the boy injured on the floor, they just carried on .................................... .

The girl tapped her foot .................................... ; her friend was late again!

He was .................................... her not to leave.

**Read Chapter 5 of *Beyond the Horizon*. Record your thoughts about each of the three questions in the spaces below.**

**The looking question is ...**
Who wanted to fight the villagers?

**The clue question is ...**
Why did the farmers run from the fields carrying their tools?

**The thinking question is ...**
How would the story be different if Sarah had not followed her father?

**Do you have any questions? Write them here.**

**Think about the conversations you have had about this text. What more have you learned? Complete the activity below.**

How has Captain Booth's opinion of Indian people changed? Why?

**Imagine you are talking to the author of *Beyond the Horizon*. Write down what you liked about the story and two things you would change.**

**Feedback**

**Do you know what the words below mean? Record your thoughts about each meaning, then look up the words in a dictionary.**

| I think this word means ... | The definition in the dictionary is ... |
|---|---|
| **sanctuary** | |
| | |
| **sheltered** | |
| | |
| **embrace** | |
| | |
| **refuge** | |
| | |
| **curious** | |
| | |

## Explore the focus word by completing the activities below.

Look up the focus word in a dictionary and write a definition.

Make up a sentence using the focus word.

**capricious**

Write a synonym for the focus word.

Write an antonym for the focus word.

**Read pages 2–11 of *The Tree*. Record your thoughts about each of the three questions in the spaces below.**

**The looking question is ...**

What activities take place in and around the tree?

**The clue question is ...**

Why is the tree so important?

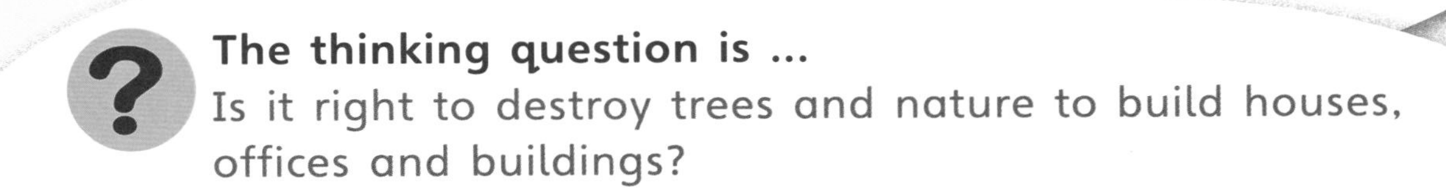

**The thinking question is ...**

Is it right to destroy trees and nature to build houses, offices and buildings?

**Do you have any questions? Write them here.**

**Think about the conversations you have had about this text. What more have you learned? Complete the activity below.**

Write an argument for the tree to remain.

**How do you think each character will feel about the plan to remove the tree to make way for a market? Write your predictions in the spaces below.**

**Feedback**

**Change each word so that it fits in the sentences. Write your answers in the spaces provided.**

**protested**

The ........................ marched through the street waving banners.

We are ........................ against the closure of public libraries.

Whenever I ask him to clean his room, he always ........................ .

**denial**

Tom kept ........................ that he had taken his sister's pencil case.

Sarah couldn't ........................ that she was tempted to eat one of the delicious-looking chocolates!

The man ........................ he had stolen the famous jewels.

**exhausted**

The runner collapsed in ........................ at the end of the marathon.

The teacher had found the school trip totally ........................ .

"Don't ........................ all your energy in the first half," suggested the football coach.

**Which words or phrases have a similar meaning to the focus word? Write them in the spaces below.**

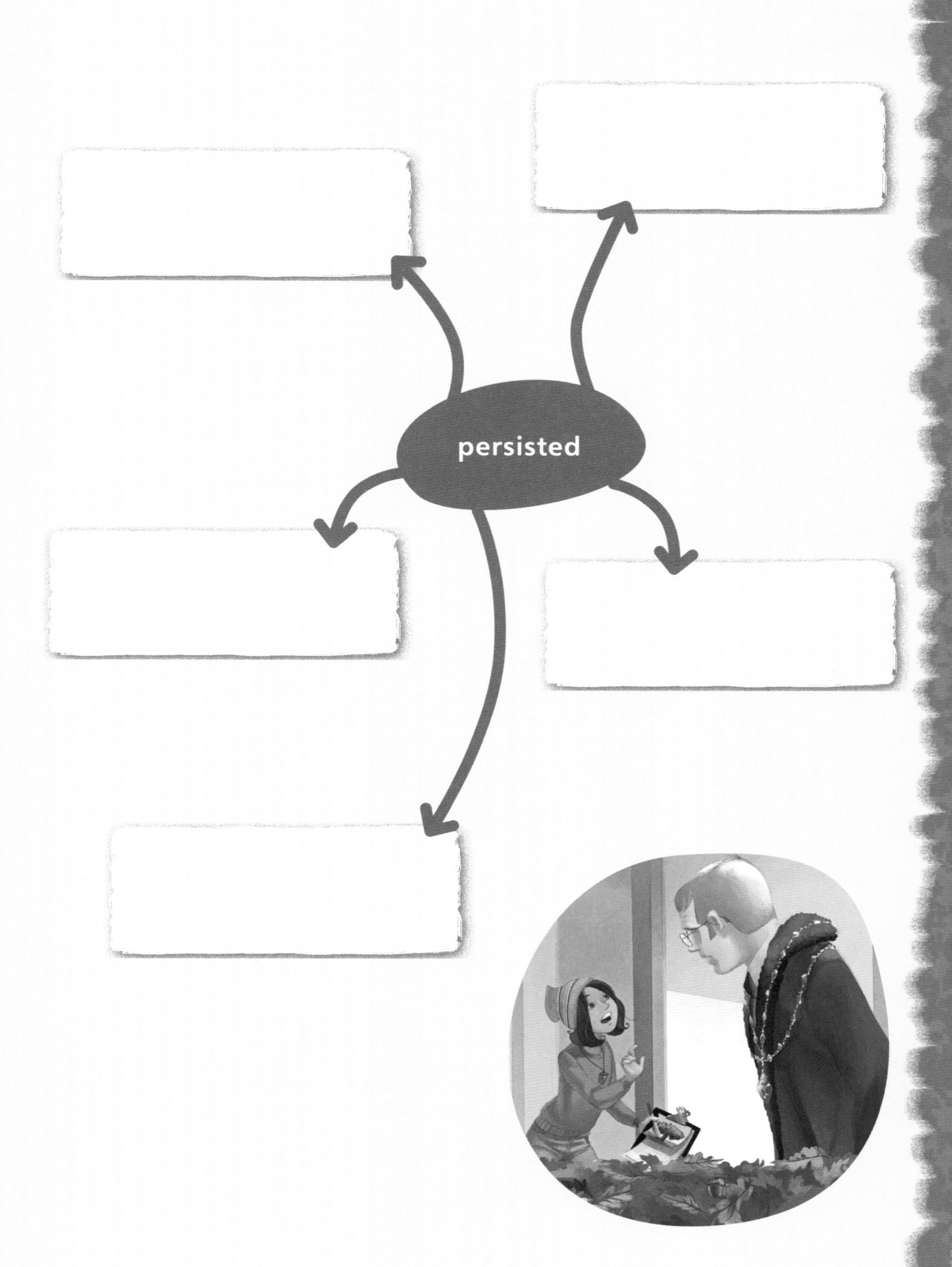

**Read pages 12–24 of *The Tree*. Record your thoughts about each of the three questions in the spaces below.**

**The looking question is …**
How does the girl try to save the tree?

**The clue question is …**
Why is the tree described as a tree of knowledge, memory and hope?

**The thinking question is …**
How do the illustrations add to the impact of the story?

**Do you have any questions? Write them here.**

**Think about the conversations you have had about this text. What more have you learned? Complete the activities below.**

Explain why the qualities of courage and perseverance are valuable.

Argue that the tree symbolises hope.

Discuss the importance of the illustrations in this text.

**Give each part of the text a mark out of 10. Write a reason for each mark in the spaces provided.**

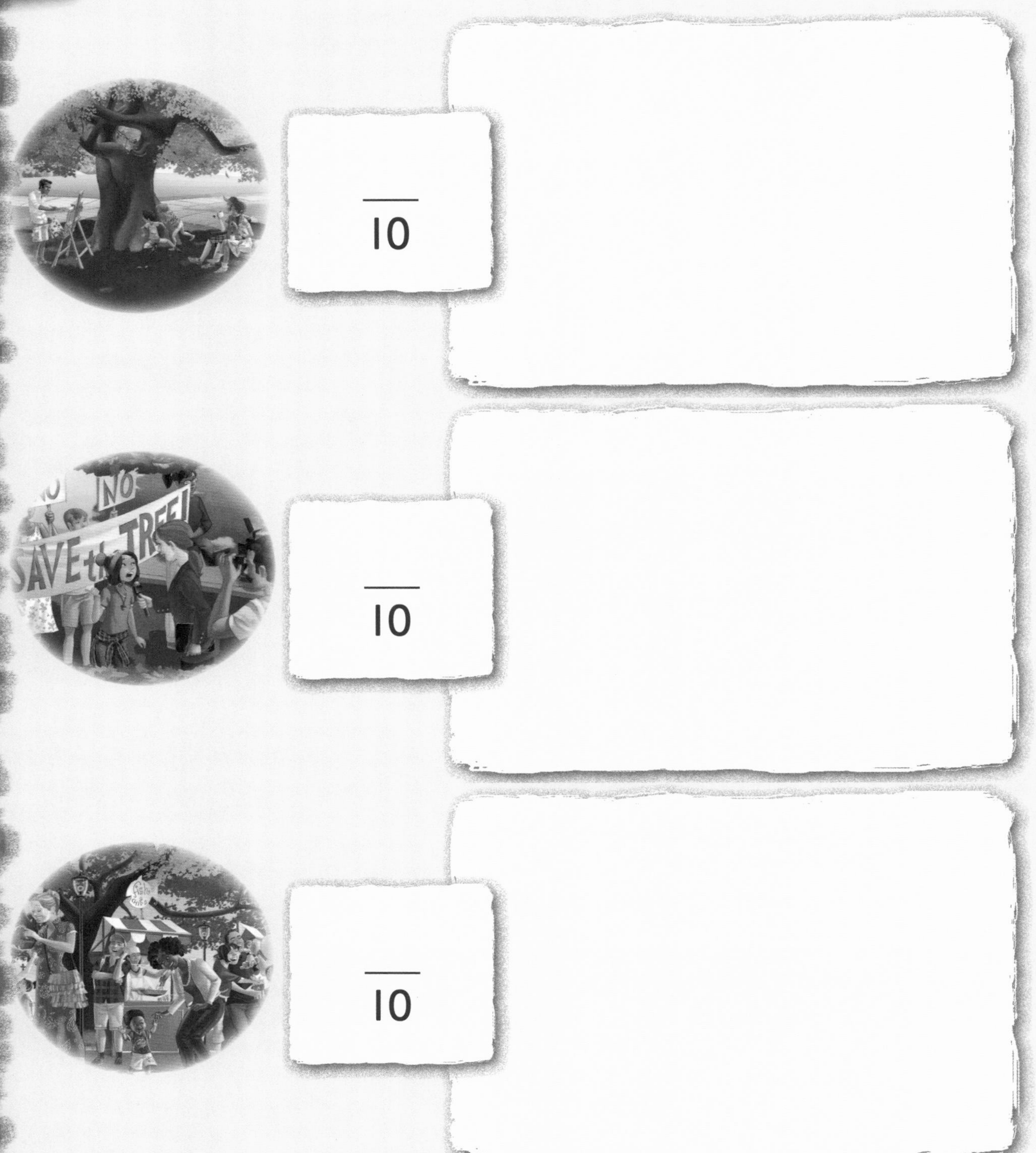


**Feedback**

## Put each word into the correct sentence.

**region** **drills** **aftershocks** **vibrations** **displaces**

**tectonic plates** **bustling** **hauling** **epicentre** **magnitude**

The ........................ of the earthquake was just a few kilometres away from the city.

The road was so bumpy that the ........................ made my teeth chatter.

Earth's ........................ make up its hard outer shell.

When Bobby's parents saw the ........................ of the mess in the house, he was grounded for a week.

After a major earthquake there will be many smaller ........................ .

Dad ........................ so much water when he gets into the bath, it drips through the ceiling.

After ........................ all the bags up the hill, Penny decided she deserved an ice cream.

There were so many people ........................ to get on the train, Mrs O'Leary was knocked over.

The Lake District is a ........................ visited by thousands of tourists each year.

Class 3F was fed up with all the fire ........................, but Mrs Fletcher explained how important it was for the children's safety.

**What can you find out about tsunamis? Complete the activities below.**

What is a tsunami?

How does a tsunami form?

tsunami

How high can a tsunami be?

Why are tsunamis dangerous?

**Read pages 4–13 of *A Tsunami Unfolds*. Record your thoughts about each of the three questions in the spaces below.**

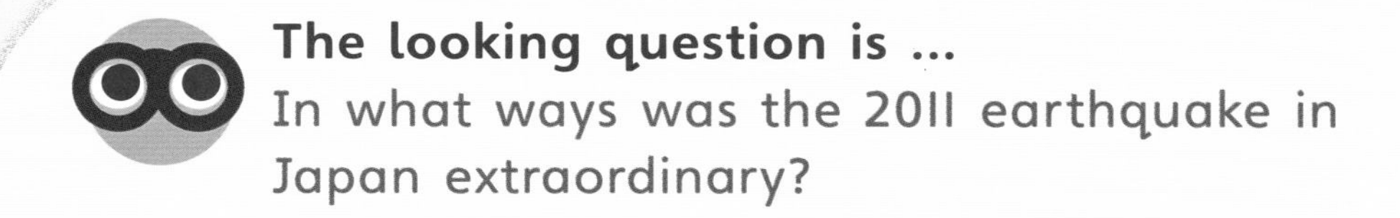

**The looking question is ...**
In what ways was the 2011 earthquake in Japan extraordinary?

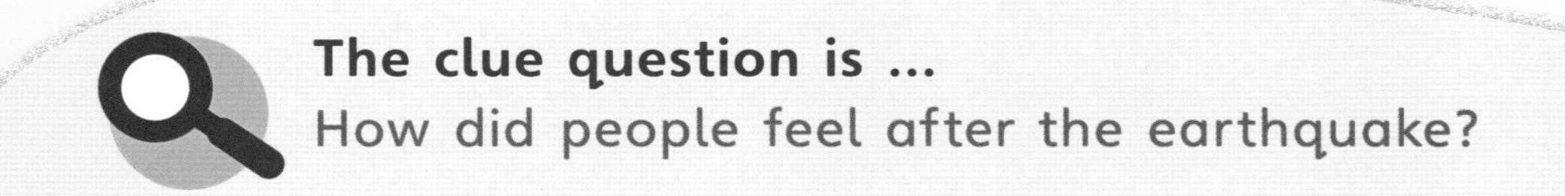

**The clue question is ...**
How did people feel after the earthquake?

**The thinking question is ...**
How have the authors created drama in this text?

**Do you have any questions? Write them here.**

**Think about the conversations you have had about this text. What more have you learned? Complete the activities below.**

Explain how you know that the people of Japan have previously experienced earthquakes.

Explain why the authors have used different text types in this book.

**What problems did the people of Japan have after the earthquake? Write your answer below. Underline evidence in the text to support your answer.**

The quake had damaged thousands of homes. It also damaged Sendai airport, and ripped pipes and lockers from walls at the Daiichi Nuclear Power Plant in Fukushima. The earthquake had knocked out electricity in many parts of Japan. With millions of people trying to use their phones, phone networks were crashing too.

**Feedback**

Do you know what the words below mean? Record your thoughts about each meaning, then look up the words in a dictionary.

| I think this word means ... | The definition in the dictionary is ... |
| --- | --- |
| **plume** | |
| | |
| **seismic** | |
| | |
| **debris** | |
| | |
| **generators** | |
| | |
| **radiation** | |
| | |

**Which words or phrases have a similar meaning to the focus word? Write them in the spaces below.**

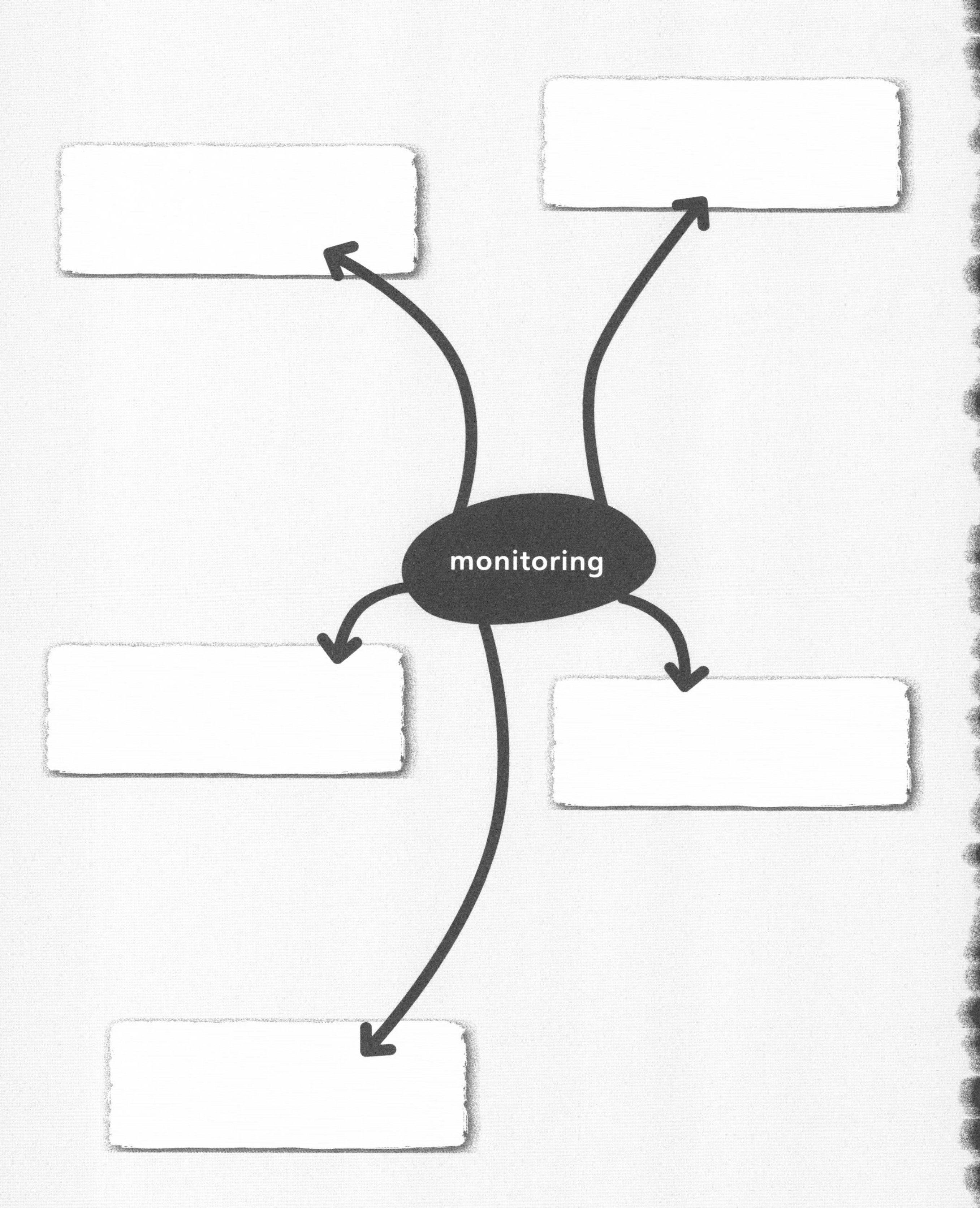

**Read pages 14–23 of *A Tsunami Unfolds*. Record your thoughts about each of the three questions in the spaces below.**

**The looking question is …**
How is the tsunami described?

**The clue question is …**
What helped to save lives during the tsunami?

**The thinking question is …**
Why do you think people choose to live in a place where tsunamis occur?

**Do you have any questions? Write them here.**

**Think about the conversations you have had about this text. What more have you learned? Complete the activities below.**

Explain how the images in the book extend your understanding.

Discuss why the authors have provided case studies from individuals.

Speculate on why some people ignored the tsunami warnings at first.

**Describe how you would feel if you were one of the people in this image. Write in the space below.**

What has happened to you?

What are you worried about?

**Feedback**

**Read the text and complete the activities below.**

Private Jones looked at the beach. It was a complete disaster zone. The cliff had collapsed, destroying the path up from the beach, and the tide had come in. A party of schoolchildren were clinging to the rocks; they were safe but with the freezing rain, they were likely to develop hypothermia. Fortunately, he and his colleagues were on a military exercise on the cliffs above the beach. They climbed down and one-by-one helped the children and their teacher to safety.

Find and copy the word that means "so cold your body starts shutting down".

Find and copy the word that means "to do with the army, navy or air force".

Find and copy the phrase that means "an area where something awful has happened".

**Change each word so that it fits in the sentences. Write your answers in the spaces provided.**

|  |  |
| --- | --- |
| **contaminated** | Please wash your hands or you will ………………………… the food. |
| | After my tummy upset we boil-washed my bedding to ………………………… it. |
| | The area around the power plant was evacuated because of the nuclear …………………………. |
| **survive** | The soldiers were ………………………… on rations of tinned food until more supplies arrived. |
| | Climbers knew that their only hope of ………………………… was to be spotted by the air rescue team. |
| | Only one ………………………… made it off the shipwrecked boat and safely to shore. |
| **assess** | Looking out the window at the rain, Mr Jones ………………………… his plans for the day. |
| | Our teacher spends a lot of time ………………………… our writing skills. |
| | After a detailed ………………………… the engineer decided that the bridge was safe. |

Read pages 24–31 of *A Tsunami Unfolds*. Record your thoughts about each of the three questions in the spaces below.

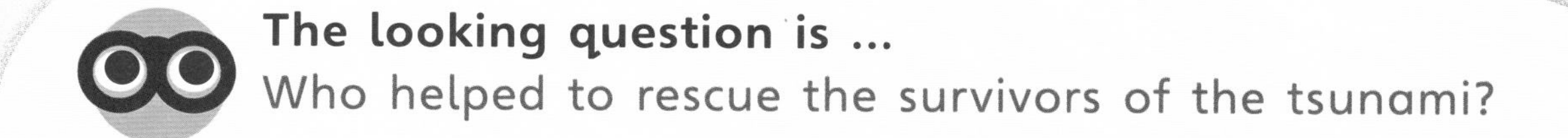

**The looking question is ...**
Who helped to rescue the survivors of the tsunami?

**The clue question is ...**
Why did some people flee from Fukushima?

**The thinking question is ...**
Why were people around the world amazed by the patience of the Japanese victims?

**Do you have any questions? Write them here.**

**Think about the conversations you have had about this text. What more have you learned? Complete the activities below.**

What do you think the survivors would say was the worst effect of the tsunami disaster?

**What were the consequences of each event in the text? Write your answers in the spaces below.**

An earthquake measuring 9.0 on the Richter scale hits Japan.

Consequence ...

A powerful tsunami with waves measuring 39 metres high sweeps the area.

Consequence ...

**Feedback**

# Reading Goals

This term I aim to ...

Find a new author I like!

Read a play with friends!

Read the book of my favourite film!

Learn a poem by heart!

# Group Discussion Rules

- We will listen carefully to the person who is speaking
- Everyone should have a chance to speak
- We will give reasons for our ideas
- We can ask others for reasons if they don't say them
- **We can agree and disagree politely with each other**
- We will respect each other's ideas and opinions
- We will share all the information in the group
- *We will try to reach an agreement together if we can*

Add any other group discussion rules your class or group has decided on here:

- ..............................
- ..............................
- ..............................
- ..............................
- ..............................

## Reading Tracker

Book title: ..................................................

Author: ..................................................

Date finished: .............................. Score out of 10 ☐

Book title: ..................................................

Author: ..................................................

Date finished: .............................. Score out of 10 ☐

Book title: ..................................................

Author: ..................................................

Date finished: .............................. Score out of 10 ☐

Book title: ..................................................

Author: ..................................................

Date finished: .............................. Score out of 10 ☐

Book title: ..................................................

Author: ..................................................

Date finished: .............................. Score out of 10 ☐

Book title: ..............................

Author: ..............................

Date finished: .............................. Score out of 10 ☐

Book title: ..............................

Author: ..............................

Date finished: .............................. Score out of 10 ☐

Book title: ..............................

Author: ..............................

Date finished: .............................. Score out of 10 ☐

Book title: ..............................

Author: ..............................

Date finished: .............................. Score out of 10 ☐

Book title: ..............................

Author: ..............................

Date finished: .............................. Score out of 10 ☐

# Read-alikes

If you liked *Beyond the Horizon*, why not try ...

Jasmine Skies
by Sita Brahmachari

Journey to the River Sea
by Eva Ibbotson

If you liked *The Tree*, why not try ...

Varmints
by Helen Ward

Follow the Moon Home
by Philippe Cousteau

If you liked *A Tsunami Unfolds*, why not try ...

Storm: The Awesome Power of Weather
by Mike Graf

Ultimate Survival Guide for Kids
by Tom Connell

# The types of text I have read this term

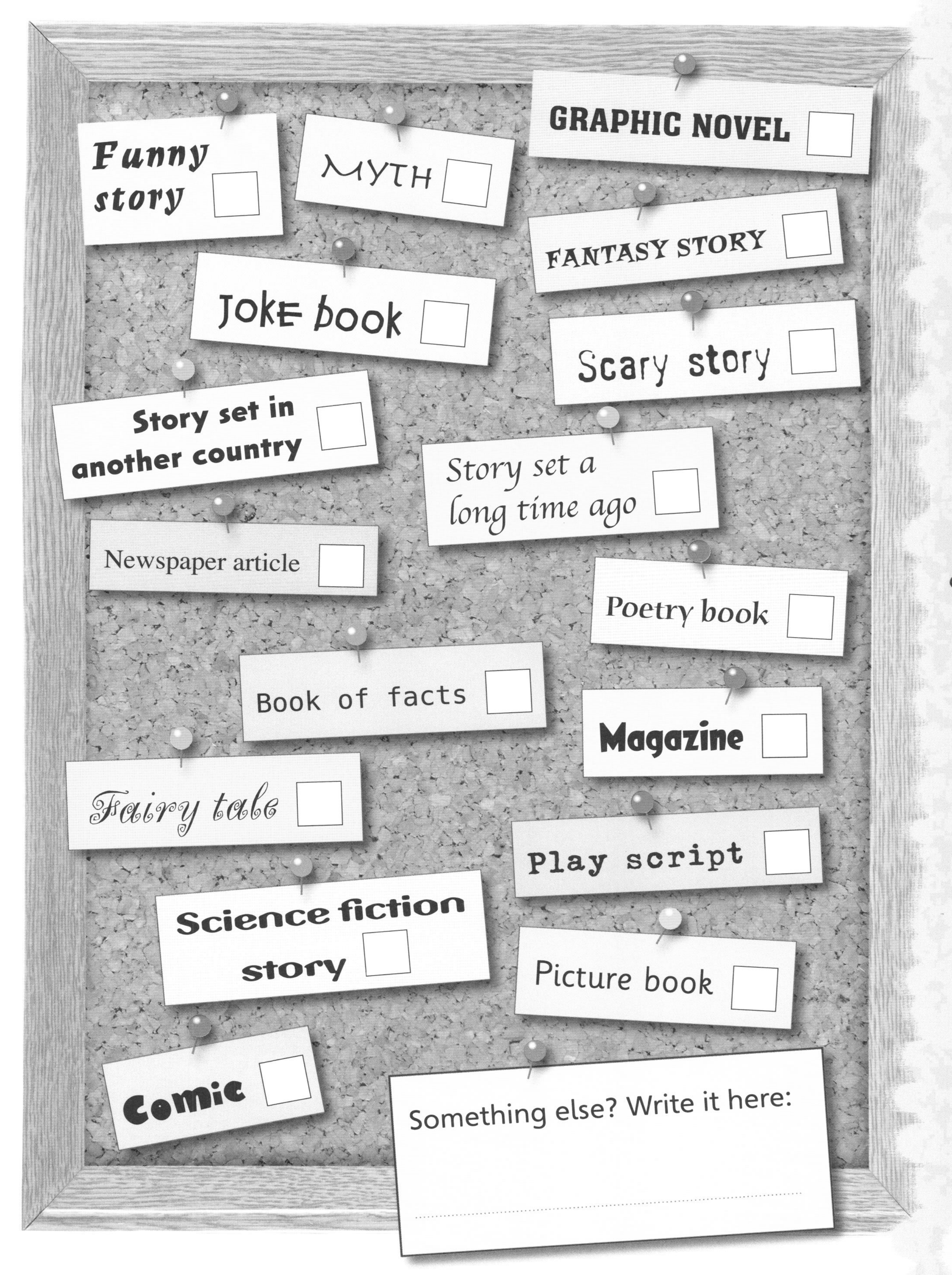

# The best new words I have learned this term

| Word | What it means |
| --- | --- |
| capricious | changeable; unpredictable |
| | |
| | |
| | |
| | |
| | |
| | |
| | |
| | |
| | |
| | |
| | |
| | |

# The best jokes I have read this term

# Reading Record

Fill in these sheets for one story you have chosen yourself.

## At the beginning

Title:

Author:

Why did you choose this book?

What score do you think you'll give it? /10

Who is the character you like most?

Has anything like this ever happened to you?

What questions do you have about the story?

What do you think will happen at the end?

## At the end

Were your predictions right?

Is there anything that still puzzles you?

What score would you give this book? /10

Who do you think would enjoy this book?

# The best facts I have read this term

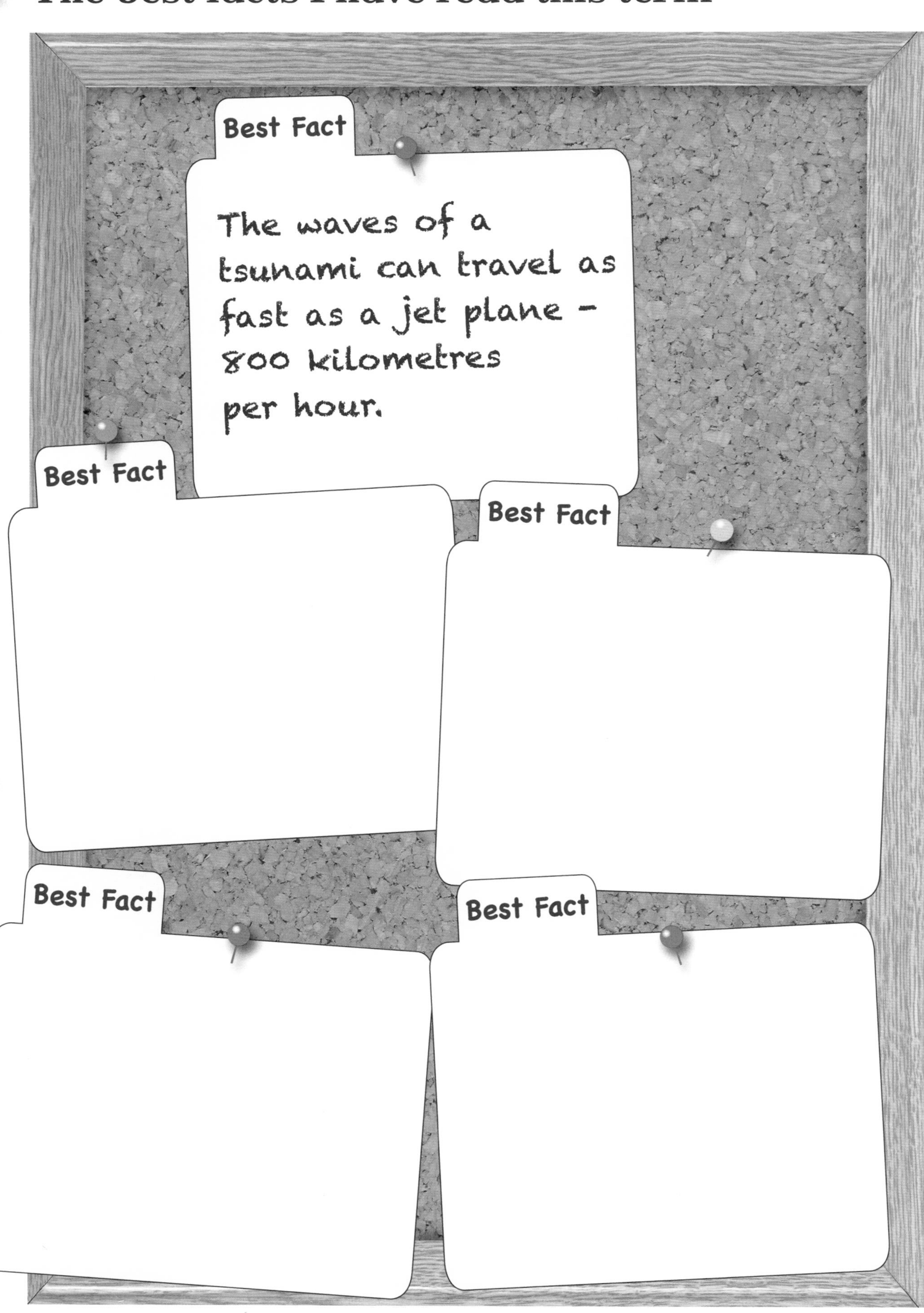

# Recommended Reads for Me

Think about someone in your group, class or family. What books would you recommend for them?

Recommended Reads for

.......................................................................................................

A story I think they'll like:

A non-fiction book I think they'll like:

A poem I think they'll like:

An author I think they'll like:

What books have been recommended for you? Write them here.

**Bug Club Comprehension is a fresh new approach that helps every child master comprehension. It uses a powerful and proven talk-based, mastery approach to help children develop a deeper understanding of texts.**

Part of the Bug Club Comprehension programme, the workbooks provide:

- activities for each day of the teaching cycle
- clear, child-friendly designs that complement the accompanying texts
- formative assessment opportunities
- a 'Reading Journal' section for children to record their independent reading.

**Series Consultants:**
Wayne Tennent and David Reedy
**Workbook and Teaching Card Authors:**
Catherine Casey, Sarah Snashall and Andy Taylor

Published by Pearson Education Limited, 80 Strand, London, WC2R 0RL.

www.pearsonschools.co.uk



Designed by Karen Awadzi, Red Giraffe

Illustrated by Victor Tavares.

First published 2017

24
15

**British Library Cataloguing in Publication Data**
A catalogue record for this book is available from the British Library

ISBN 978 0 435 18655 5



Printed in the UK by Bell and Bain Ltd.

**Acknowledgements**
The publisher would like to thank the following for their kind permission to reproduce their photographs in this workbook and accompanying photocopiable activities:

**Alamy Images:** Aflo Co., Ltd. PCM_19b, epa european pressphoto agency b.v. 46, PCM_17, PCM_18, jeremy sutton-hibbert 50, Mark Pearson 51b, PCM_19c, PCM_20b, ZUMA Press, Inc. 51t, PCM_19t, PCM_20c; **Shutterstock.com:** Robbi 57, 62

**Cover images:** *Front:* **Alamy Images:** jeremy sutton-hibbert



www.pearsonschools.co.uk
enquiries@pearson.com

ISBN 978-0-435-18655-5

9 780435 186555